Silly Joke Books

SILLY JOKES
ABOUT
BUGS

by Michael Dahl

PEBBLE
a capstone imprint

Published by Pebble, an imprint of Capstone
1710 Roe Crest Drive, North Mankato, Minnesota 56003
capstonepub.com

Copyright © 2022 by Capstone. All rights reserved. No part of this publication may be reproduced in whole or in part, or stored in a retrieval system, or transmitted in any form or by any means, electronic, mechanical, photocopying, recording, or otherwise, without written permission of the publisher.

Library of Congress Cataloging-in-Publication Data is available on the Library of Congress website.
ISBN: 9781977131591 (hardcover)
ISBN: 9781977154842 (ebook PDF)

Summary: A collection of jokes about bugs for young readeres.

Editorial Credits
Editor: Christianne Jones; Designer: Brann Garvey and Mighty Media; Media Researcher: Jo Miller; Production Specialist: Laura Manthe

Image Credits
Shutterstock: 2happy, Cover, mantis, aleks1949, 20, mammoth, BEJITA, 16, termites, Claudio Divizia, 11, moon, Daniel Prudek, 4, bees, 23, bees, Dario Sabljak, 18, drum set, Dudarev Mikhail, 10, ocean, Eric Isselee, 18, mantises, exopixel, 21, sunglasses, Fer Gregory, 15, background, genky, 14, light bulb, 15, light bulbs, Happy monkey, 17, bunny, Helga Chirk, 7, Ilya Andriyanov, 6, irin-k, Cover, ladybug, fly, 9, ant, 12, fly, Kadak, 4, bus, khlungcenter, 3, 19, firefly, 24, Kletr, 11, tick, Lamyai, 23, ants, Lepas, 17, honeycomb, MaleWitch, 12, shoes, MaraZe, 16, oatmeal, Mehmet Gokhan Bayhan, 10, laptop, Mizkit, Cover, microphone, NAN728, 9, charts, New Africa, 13, shoes, 14, clock, otello-stpdc, 9, laptop, Paul Looyen, 10, spider, Pixel-Shot, 12, shoes, 13, shoes, Protasov AN, 17, wings, pun483, 20, wings, Sergiy1975, 18, guitar, sevenke, 8, 21, book, souloff, design element, sruilk, 11, ticks, Stock High angle view, 19, track, Suzanne Tucker, 21, firefly, Valentina Proskurina, 5, Vitawin, 18, drum sticks, WhiteJack, 11, spring, yod67, 13, centipede

All internet sites appearing in back matter were available and accurate when this book was sent to press.

Printed and bound in China. 5404

Table of Contents

Buzzy Buddies 4

Crazy Crawlies 8

Bunches Of Bugs 14

Activity: Bug Hunt 22

Glossary 23

Read More 23

Internet Sites 24

Index .... HELLO! 24

BUZZY BUDDIES

How do bees get to school?

They take the school buzz.

How do bees brush their hair?

They use a honeycomb.

What goes zzub zzub?

A bee buzzing backward.

Where do bees go after they are married?

On their honeymoon.

What did the bee say when it was hot outside?

"Swarm here, isn't it?"

What do you call a bee that can't make up its mind?

A maybee.

What's the smartest insect?

A spelling bee.

Where do you find a bee's stinger?

On its bee-hind.

WHOOP, THERE IT IS!

CRAZY CRAWLIES

What do you call a 100-year-old ant?

Antique.

HAHA! HEHE!

What's the biggest ant in the world?

An eleph-ANT.

What kind of ant loves numbers?

An accountant.

Why did the spider take its computer to the beach?

So it could surf the web.

What do you call insects that live on the moon?

Luna-ticks.

HOME SWEET MOON!

What's green and jumps a mile per minute?

A grasshopper with hiccups.

BOING!

BOING!

What is a bedbug's favorite season?

Spring.

What do you call a fly without wings?

A walk.

What do you call spiders that just got married?

Newly-webs.

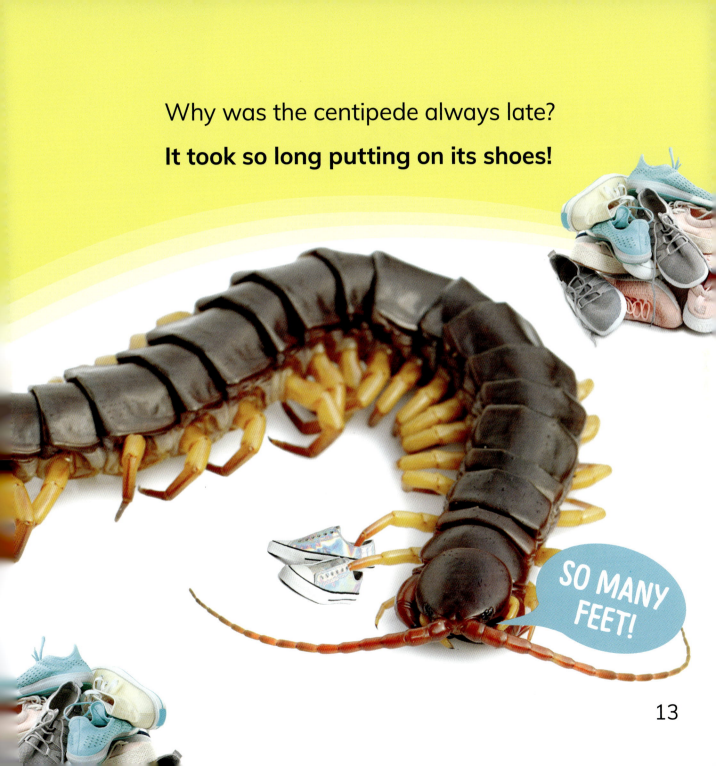

Why was the centipede always late?

It took so long putting on its shoes!

SO MANY FEET!

BUNCHES OF BUGS

Why did the spider buy a car?

So it could take it for a spin.

What insects live inside a clock?

Ticks.

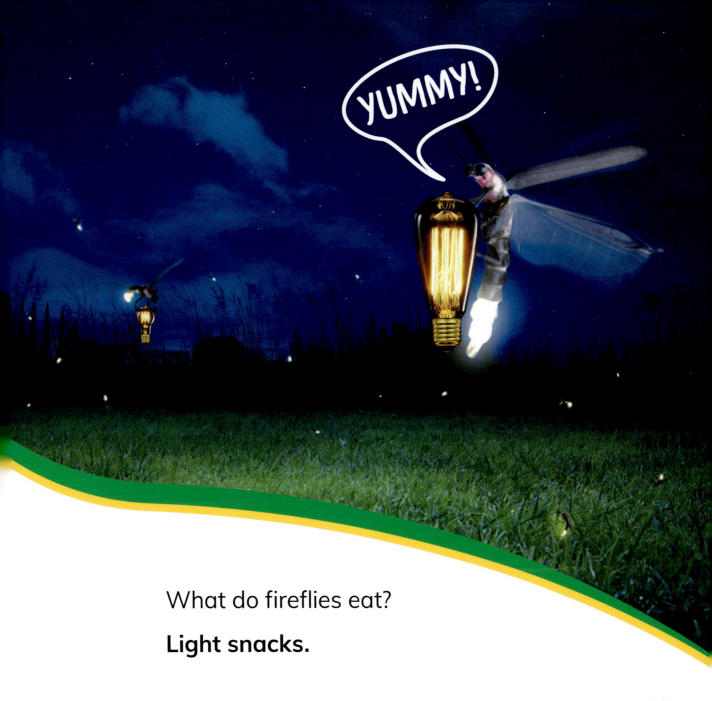

What do fireflies eat?

Light snacks.

What did the termites eat for breakfast?

Oak-meal.

What did the termites eat for lunch?

Wooden you like to know.

How can you tell when flies are famous actors?

When you see them on the screen.

What do you get if you combine a bee and a bunny?

A honey bunny.

What do you call a musical insect?

A humbug.

Why couldn't the butterfly go to the dance?

It was a moth ball.

How do fireflies start a race?

"Ready, set, glow!"

What is the biggest moth in the world?

A mammoth.

What insects are the best students?

Fireflies. They are the brightest.

What did the firefly say when she was leaving?

"Got to glow!"

ACTIVITY: BUG HUNT

What you need:
- paper
- pencil
- scissors
- markers, crayons, or colored pencils

What you do:

1. Go on a funny bug hunt! Cut the paper into six pieces.

2. Draw a bug on one side of the paper.

3. On the other side of the paper, write a joke about the bug. You can either write your own joke or use one from this book.

4. Repeat steps 2 and 3 for each piece of paper.

5. Hide the bugs around the house and have someone find them.

GLOSSARY

famous (FAY-muss)—well known, popular

hive (HIVE)—a round, papery nest where bees live

insect (IN-sekt)—a small animal with a hard outer shell, six legs, three body sections, and two antennae; most insects have wings.

termite (TUR-mahyt)—an antlike insect that eats wood

READ MORE

Dahl, Michael. *Michael Dahl's BIG Book of Jokes.* North Mankato, MN: Capstone, 2020.

Pellowski, Michael J. *Mega-funny Jokes & Riddles.* New York: Sterling, 2017.

Riddle, H.A. *The Best of Laugh Yourself Silly Jokes for Kids.* Tucson, AZ: Lonotek, 2018.

INTERNET SITES

Enchanted Learning
www.enchantedlearning.com/jokes/animals/bugs.shtml

Funology
www.funology.com/bug-and-insectjokes

THE END

INDEX

ants, 8, 9
bedbugs, 11
bees, 4, 5, 6, 17
butterflies, 18
centipedes, 13
fireflies, 15, 19, 21

flies, 12, 16
grasshoppers, 11
moths, 18, 20
spiders, 10, 12, 14
termites, 16
ticks, 11, 14